Meret Oppenheim

The Loveliest Vowel Empties:

Collected Poems

Translated from German and French
by Kathleen Heil

 WORLD POETRY

The Loveliest Vowel Empties: Collected Poems of Meret Oppenheim
Copyright © Suhrkamp, 2015, 2023
Original-language texts published with permission from Suhrkamp
English translation copyright © Kathleen Heil, 2023
Introduction copyright © Kathleen Heil, 2023

First Edition, First Printing, 2023
ISBN 978-1-954218-08-6

World Poetry Books
New York, NY
www.worldpoetrybooks.com

Distributed in the US by SPD/Small Press Distribution
www.spdbooks.org

Distributed in the UK and Europe by Turnaround Publisher Services
www.turnaround-uk.com

Library of Congress Control Number: 2022948953

Cover image by Meret Oppenheim, "X-Ray of M.O.'s Skull"
(Röntgenaufnahme des Schädels M.O.), 1964, printed 1981.
Gelatin silver print. Publisher: Levy Galerie, Hamburg, 1970. Edition: 20.
The Museum of Modern Art, New York, NY. (Acquired through the generosity
of Marlene Hess and James D. Zirin.) Digital Image ©
The Museum of Modern Art/Licensed by SCALA / Art Resource, NY
Image © 2022 Artists Rights Society (ARS), New York / ProLitteris, Zurich

Cover design by Andrew Bourne
Typesetting by Don't Look Now
Printed in Lithuania by KOPA

The work of the translator was supported by a grant of the German
Translators' Fund as part of the programme NEUSTART KULTUR by the
Federal Government Commissioners for Culture and Media.

World Poetry Books is committed to publishing exceptional translations of
poetry from a broad range of languages and traditions, bringing the work of
modern masters, emerging voices, and pioneering innovators from around the
world to English-language readers in affordable trade editions. Founded in
2017, World Poetry Books is a 501(c)(3) nonprofit and charitable organization
based in New York City and affiliated with the Humanities Institute and the
Translation Program at the University of Connecticut (Storrs).

Table of Contents

Introduction

> When nature is no longer treated as an enemy to humanity, and the bat-
> tle of the sexes is consigned to history because the so-called feminine
> qualities possessed equally by men—feeling, sensing, intuition—have
> been fully integrated, when the significance of woman's contribution to
> the preservation and development of human society has been properly
> recognized, when comfort is no longer mistaken for culture, when once
> again there is a need for beauty: then, poetry and art will automatically
> come back into their own, even if the veil of longing rests over them,
> always, like an eternal promise.
>
>   — *Meret Oppenheim*
>   *(from a lecture at the Federal Institute*
>   *of Technology in Zurich, 1983)*

MERET OPPENHEIM'S BODY OF WORK integrates what human soci-
ety could not in her lifetime, and what it certainly has yet to do
adequately in ours. Born in 1913 in Berlin-Charlottenburg to a
German Jewish father and Swiss mother, she lived out the initial
decades of her life in the shadows of Europe's two world wars.
As yet another war rages on, I think of the hope inherent in her
audacious artistic practice, which spanned painting, sculpture,
works on paper, jewelry design, and poetry—hope evidenced by
the book you hold in your hands now, the first volume in English
translation to collect her poetry in its entirety. Hope inherent, not
because Oppenheim's work is particularly uplifting, much less
cheery; indeed, the language in her verse is often exceedingly dark
and piercing. But her inventive verse, in expanding æsthetic and
imaginative possibility, opens up spaces for transformation—even
under circumstances where these spaces are veiled by cruelty, and

are therefore fleeting. Such contradictions come to life in the untitled poem that opens, in my translation, with the exclamation "Freedom!":

> Freedom!
> Finally!
> The harpoons fly
> A rainbow encamps on the streets
> Undermined only by the distant buzz of giant bees.

Despite its flights of fancy, the poem suffers no illusions, ending, "(Wind and shrieking in the distance.)"

Dark imagery is present throughout the collection, and much has been made of Oppenheim's nearly two-decade-long artistic crisis, as she herself defined the period from 1937 to 1954 during which she destroyed or left unfinished many of her artworks. But I don't think of Oppenheim's work as truly dark, if by that one means cynical or despairing. I wonder if it isn't possible to shift the personal to the social, to consider that Oppenheim came up in Paris in the 1930s as a woman among (older, established) men: the artists in her milieu—André Breton, Man Ray, Marcel Duchamp, Max Ernst—were all about twenty years her senior. She also became citizen of a country, Switzerland, in which men didn't cede women the right to vote at a federal level until 1971 (and one tiny canton, Appenzell Inner-Rhodes, didn't do so at a local level until a federal mandate forced the shift, in 1990). She herself singled out the weight of such realities: "I felt as if millennia of discrimination against women were resting on my shoulders, as if embodied in my feelings of inferiority."

Alongside the limitations she had to endure as a woman artist among men was the reality of violence and war. In a prescient poem from 1934:

Weak and weaker to the left.
Same for the living.
The dead, straight ahead,

Who can help but think of the horrors of the Nazi project? Amid their rise to power, Oppenheim's father was forced to cease his medical practice in Germany and return to Switzerland. "Do you hear the lions roaring / United exiled exhausted," Oppenheim writes in one poem; in another, written in 1943 after the bombings of Milan:

along the sky's edge
wavelike lighting looms:
anguish and menace—
is anyone calling for help?
A valley rife with flashes
beyond the mountains.

And then there is the indelible, comically savage image of brown dogs on a ship that

stick their necks out beyond the railing, clutching
small knives in their mouths, which they let drop
from time to time on the people down below. The knives
transfix the sun stranded on the
ocean floor. The sun is growing
little fins.

The language of her poems occupies a "peculiar continent," one marked by pain but set, nevertheless, "in bright relief." A poem, for example, is "provoked / by twiddling a little wad of cotton / around my fingers."

And so, amid the darkness there is still space for whimsy in the poems. One of my favorites has her numbering the noses of shadows that are "Squabbling over old bread / And clucking like chickens."

OPPENHEIM ASSERTED HER INDEPENDENCE in life and verse. "Whoosh! The loveliest vowel empties," she writes, a line from a poem that was also the title of a painting she gave Max Ernst upon dumping him: *Husch, Husch, der schönste Vokal entleert sich* (in English the painting has been given the descriptive title *Quick, Quick, the Most Beautiful Vowel is Voiding* by art historians). And it didn't occur to me until just now—*pace* Alfred Jarry—that the English idiom, *to dump*, nicely mirrors *sich entleeren* as a reflexive verb that can be used to refer to emptying or evacuating one's bladder or bowels.

Which brings us to the matter of literary translation. Wherefore "whoosh," and who am I to change Oppenheim's words? Certain readers might cry out, balking at my carrying over the "gelben Wellen" as "mauve waves." Translation is always transformation, and attempts to create descriptive literary translations—sometimes erroneously called "literal" ones—are best avoided. Which does not mean that a translator seeking to create equivalent effects is making decisions without regard for what's on the page. Sensitivity and respect go hand in hand with the task—alongside, of course, attention to meaning and connotation. But true respect in translation also calls for seizing freedom from the language one is working with, whose syntax, punctuation, and prosody are systems independent of—even if ancillary to—the language one is translating into.

So, in Oppenheim's poetry, which is often driven by sound to build (associative) sense, "Schädlich sind die Nebenmotten" becomes "Baneful are the additional suns"—where *Nebenmotten* (the invented compound "additionalmoths") calls to mind

Nebenkosten (a "real" word in German referring to one's monthly or utility bills). The English translation transforms these "additional sums" into suns. The seven-eight-nine numerical pun of "Er wird gesiebt, geachtet / Und neun und gut geschlachtet" becomes "They'll be severed, attended, / Nine and well butchered." The violence of the lines comes in slightly earlier with the near homophone of *seven*, forgoing the descriptive *screened*—but, since one can also "sever ties" by means of separation, this choice felt necessary to bind the verb to the numerical sequence. In another poem, the German word for deadly nightshade, Tollkirschen, suggests an invented composite word for "goodchurches," leading Oppenheim to imagine that "forgiveness and vilification / come and go and clap their hands." Here, I opted for the evocations of the plant itself, deadly nightshade, followed by "goodcherries," a descriptive translation of the composite noun that carries that churchy *ch-* sound.

Because no two languages are alike, creating effective correspondences in literary translation is always a matter of substitution, addition, or subtraction to render an equivalent effect. In "Self-portrait from 50,000 B.C. to X," Oppenheim makes full use of the natural plasticity of German to glue together nouns in the service of creating new ones. She writes of a "Geistkugel" or "spiritsphere"—but "Kugel" can also be used colloquially to refer to a scoop of ice cream, a ball, or a bullet—it is punchier than the demure "sphere," which means the word is normalized slightly in my translation. So, in the line preceding, where an awkward passive voice would occur in a descriptive translation of "Alle / Gedanken, die je gedacht wurden" (descriptively: "all thoughts that have ever been thought"), a scoop of that playfulness has been introduced and I've translated the phrase as: "Each and every / thought that has ever been thunk," with that nonstandard past participle thunking in to brighten up the syntax.

OPPENHEIM BEGAN WRITING POEMS not long after moving to Paris in 1932 at the age of 18, where she lived for several years and later returned frequently. Oppenheim left all but a handful of her poems untitled, and the bulk of her poetic output took place from 1933 to 1944, though she also wrote several poems in later decades—including "Self-Portrait from 50,000 B.C. to X," her last recorded work, written in 1980, five years before her death. Seven of the forty-nine poems collected here Oppenheim wrote in French and then translated herself into German; both languages were consulted when rendering my versions in English. Her poems exist in conversation with the French Symbolists, whose work was, of course, a lodestar for Breton and the Surrealists in general. Think of the fairies that appear in her poems, "flying by with bright thighs," along with the shadows in the woods, the fur, and the clover, all of which recall imagery present in Rimbaud's *Illuminations*. Though the first exhibition of her work was at the 1933 edition of the Salon des Surindépendants alongside established Surrealist artists, in later decades Oppenheim chose to distance herself from this limiting label, and the 2022 transatlantic retrospective of her work, "My Exhibition," rightly situates her oeuvre in the context of its own singularity.

But let's return to the "whoosh!" of the title poem and the matter of sound in her poetry in general, the way the "loveliest vowel empties." This perfectly pithy three-line poem builds its prosody through repetition and assonance. "Whoosh" came in with the sounds of "worship" and "shoe," an onomatopoeic exclamation that empties itself of its vowel. The lips purse, evacuating air in the throat to produce the *o* sound. As concerns those "gelben Wellen," it was clear to me that the waves needed to be mauve and not yellow in order to echo the perfect rhyme with one made slant. In one of her most sonically distinctive poems ("East winches east..."), one "knows and noirs at little"—"weiß und weiß an wenig." Here, Oppenheim plays with the fact that *weiß* is both the German word for "white" and a conjugation of the verb *wissen*, meaning "to know."

The late North American poet C.D. Wright famously said, "It is a function of poetry to locate those zones inside us that would be free, and declare them so." I can't help but think of this phrase in conversation with Oppenheim's most oft-cited declaration: "Nobody will give you freedom—you have to seize it." Though Wright's life and work couldn't have been more different from Oppenheim's, both women point to the way in which, when they "come back into their own," poetry and art expand possibility, even (and perhaps especially) amid dire conditions.

The enduring legacy of Oppenheim's poetry is her capacity for lyric—and lyrically rendered—transformations that refuse to refuse harsh realities. In one poem, she has the wind blowing black banks across a body of water, upending Brecht's astute interrogation as to why we call the rushing river violent but not the banks that restrain it. Oppenheim, in her poetry, makes words a *whoosh* and shakes them loose. "The black sack is full" she observes in another poem, and yet, "fireworks pop and the night is sequinstrewn."

Kathleen Heil
Berlin, July 2022

The Loveliest Vowel Empties

———

Von Beeren nährt man sich
Mit dem Schuh verehrt man sich
Husch, husch, der schönste Vokal entleert sich.

———

We feed on berries
We worship with the shoe
Whoosh! The loveliest vowel empties.

———

Endlich!
Die Freiheit!
Die Harpunen fliegen.

Der Regenbogen lagert in den Straßen,
Nur noch vom fernen Summen der Riesenbienen unterhöhlt.

Alle verlieren alles, das sie, ach wie oft,
Vergeblich überflogen hatte.

Aber:

   Genoveva:

Steif
Auf dem Kopfe stehend
Zwei Meter über der Erde
Ohne Arme.

Ihr Sohn Schmerzereich:
In ihr Haar gewickelt.

Mit den Zähnen bläst
sie ihn über sich her!

Kleine Fontäne.

Ich wiederhole: Kleine Fontäne.
(Wind und Schreie von ferne.)

Freedom!
Finally!
The harpoons fly.

A rainbow encamps on the streets,
Undermined only by the distant buzz of giant bees.

Everyone loses everything—as she, as ever,
Buzzed past in vain.

But:

   Genevieve:

Stiff
Standing on her head
Two meters above the ground
Armless.

Her son Schmerzereich:
Unbearably swaddled in her hair.

With her teeth she blows
him off and away!

Little fountain.

I repeat: Little fountain.
(Wind and shrieking in the distance.)

Wenn Sie mir das Richtige nennen, kann ich
Ihnen das Lob vom Raben mit den veränderlichen
und schillernden Füßen singen.
Am liebsten sind mir diese kalten Lachblumen
und ihre Winke, deren Schatten im Dunkeln
leuchten.

Wer nimmt den Wahnsinn von den Bäumen?
Wen beschenkt der Himmel mit Dampfveilchen?
Wie rät ein Untergang dem nächsten?

Diese und andere Fragen werden so gelöst:
Man trenne den Duft von seiner Fahrt und
versuche sein Ohr im Lauf um eine Meile
zu schürzen. Jetzt kann die Luft ihre Grenzen
um zwei Grad verengen, und das Ergebnis läßt nicht
auf sich warten.

If you tell me the right one to name, I can
sing the praises of the raven
with the ever-changing, opalescent feet.
I like best the cold laughing flowers
with their nodding, their shadows glowing
in the dark.

Who thieves madness from the trees?
Who have the heavens showered with hazy violets?
How does one demise advise the next?

These and other questions are resolved like this:
you cleave the scent from your journey,
aiming your ear along the run to gather up
one mile. The air can now narrow its limits
by two degrees. The results are not long
in coming.

Die Schreie der Hunde steigen
Sie bleiben stehen
Mit starren Hälsen
Aber ihre Schreie steigen.

The bellowing of the dogs looms
They are stilled
By stiff necks
But their bellows loom.

Mit Blumen und Blüten

Wer auch mit den Spangen eilt:
Immer wird das Licht ihn spalten.
Aber nie kann man ihn fassen,
Lebend oder tot ihn halten.

Of Blood and Blooms

Whoever's quick with the lure
Will always be cleaved by the light
But can never be caught,
Found dead or alive.

Für dich – wider dich
Wirf alle Steine hinter dich
Und laß die Wände los.

An dich – auf dich
Für hundert Sänger über sich
Die Hufe reißen los.

ICH weide meine Pilze aus
ICH bin der erste Gast im Haus
Und laß die Wände los.

For you, against you
Throw all the stones behind you
And let fall the walls.

At you, upon you
The hooves tear loose
For a hundred singers above.

I gut my mushrooms
I am the first guest come through
And let fall the walls.

Soviel wie wach im Schlafe sehen hören

Astor sah ihn im Schlafe hören. Er beobachtete ihn einige
Zeit mit den Augen, – um sich dann um so schneller in
den Wind unter dem blühenden Rosenstrauch zu legen,
so schnell, daß er seine künstlichen Ohren erst nach
einiger Zeit aus der entgegengesetzten Richtung wieder
auf sich zukommen sah. Er nahm es ihnen aber nicht übel
und befestigte sie, nach kurzem Nachdenken, an dem
letzten Brief seiner Mutter oder am knorrigen Stamm des
Rockefeller Buildings. Als er die Augen erhob, sah er, daß
sich ein paar Fenster aus dem Hause gebeugt hatten und ihm
Zeichen machten. Obwohl er wußte, daß der Igel im Innern
des Hauses immer dicker wurde und seine Borsten die Haut
des guten Kindes zu ritzen begannen, so hatte er doch bis
jetzt geglaubt, daß dieser davor zurückschrecken werde, die
Fenster in die Wüste und in den offenen Rachen des Aetna
zu jagen. Da – schon fielen die ersten Tropfen, und ein
Fenster nach dem andern entstieg seiner sterblichen Hülle
unter Zurücklassung von mindestens einer Schiffsladung
Vogelmist. Astor bedeckte sich mit einem durchsichtigen
Maulwurfshügel und begab sich ungesehen an die Stätte des
Unglücks.

Viravorabilis:

In Gedanken versunken hatte sich Astor seinem Heim
genähert. Er legte sich nieder und schlief bald ein. Als
er am andern Tag erwachte, hing er auf einem fremden
Kleiderbügel. In der Tasche fand er eine Visitenkarte, auf der
sein neuer Name gedruckt stand: Caroline.

As though awake while asleep seeing hearing

Asleep Astor saw him hearing. With his eyes for some time he observed him—only to swiftly lie down beneath the blossoming rosebush in the wind, so swiftly that it took awhile for him to see his artificial ears again approaching him from the opposite direction. He didn't hold it against them, however, and after quick consideration fastened them to his mother's last letter or to the gnarled trunk of the Rockefeller Center. When he looked up, he saw that a few windows were leaning out of the building, signaling to him. Although he knew that the hedgehog inside the building was growing fatter, its bristles beginning to scratch the good child's skin, until now he had always believed that the former would balk at chasing the windows into the desert and into Mount Aetna's open maw. There, the first drops began to fall and one window after another alighted from its mortal remains, leaving behind no less than a shipload of bird shit. Astor took cover in an invisible molehill, proceeding sight unseen to the scene of the catastrophe.

Viravorabilis:

Lost in thought, Astor made his way back home. He lay down and quickly fell asleep. When he woke the next day, he found himself hanging on an unfamiliar coat hanger. In the pocket he found a calling card, printed with his new name: Caroline.

———

Elle me tend sa ceinture
brillante
comme une sauterelle
à travers les mers
loin de son île.

———

Sie hält mir ihren Gürtel hin
schimmernd
wie eine Heuschrecke
über die Meere
fern ihrer Insel.

―

She offers me her belt
glistening
like a grasshopper
far from her island
beyond the seas.

—

Osten Winden Osten
Die Ebene will rosten
Verlegen und Vergißmeinnicht
In vielen Wagen hängt man nicht
Trotz weiß und weiß an wenig
Trotz rotem Stein am Lebenslicht
Anstelle Sieb und König
Nur wer die Rädermuse liebt
Hat Weiß und Sieb und König

—

East winches east
The plains will creak
Flitting and forget-me-not
In many carts one does not horse
Though knows and noirs at little
Though red stone in the lifelight
In lieu of sieve and king
Only those who love the wheelmuse
Have noirs and sieve and king

———

Und kommen sie am Abend
Am Morgen kommen sie nicht
An jedem leisen Raben
Zerbricht ja ihr Gesicht.

Nie wird sich das Unglück enthüllen, das, ohne sich um
die Syllabel zu kümmern, in das reizende Städtchen R.
einbrach.

Ruhig nagten die Narzissen, und die Dächer waren gut
gedeckt. Bürger, Bauer und Bettelmann schliefen. Als um
2 h nachmittags die Helden anstürmten, wagte niemand,
ihnen ihr Monogramm zu entreißen.

Ohne auf Widerstand zu stoßen, drangen sie vor, bis sie den
Ausblick auf das unendliche Domino hatten.

They come in the evening
In the morning they don't
Her face made craven
By every silent raven.

The misfortune that descended on the charming village of R.
(without worrying over the syllables) will never be revealed.

The daffodils quietly festered, the roofs were secured. The
villagers, peasants, and beggars slept. When heroes rushed
in at two in the afternoon, no one dared make off with their
monogram.

They advanced without encountering any resistance until
they had a view of the never-ending domino.

———

Une dame dans la quarantaine, modestement
habillée, qui fabrique des pièces rouges
et argent qui ont du chocolat à l'intérieur.
C'est elle qui a écrit un traité sur les
souris blanches faites en »R«.

———

Eine Dame in den Vierzigern,
unauffällig gekleidet,
die rote und silberne Münzen herstellt
die innen aus Schokolade sind.
Sie hat eine Abhandlung geschrieben über
die weißen Mäuse aus »R«.

A lady in her forties, simply dressed,
who manufactures red and silver coins
made of chocolate inside.
She's the one who wrote a treatise on
the white mice made in "R."

Lieber nichts als etwas man soll nicht schön tun aber
Dem Wasser seinen Fall lassen
Weder reifen die Nüsse noch tragen die Katzen ihre
Schwänze zu Grabe oh nein oh nein glaube nichts
Sondern verdamme ohne zu urteilen
Fern sind die Berge sie starren mit ihren felsigen
Kuppen zarte Finger streichen darüber und jedes
Zeichen von Liebe wird von den Vögeln fortgetragen
Wohin so wie die Steine übereinanderlagern
So liegen die Eisenbahnen in ihren Höhlen
Viel hört man nicht aber es genügt
In regelmäßigen Abständen ziehen sie tiefe Züge
Aus ihren Rohren und stoßen Wasserschwälle aus
Die sich über die Wiesen ergießen
Und die Kuckucksuhr schlägt drei aber nichts
Geschieht nur ein paar Kugeln springen aus
Dem Feuer Gott vergelts es gibt immer noch
Tollkirschen wo Verzeihung und Verleumdung
Aus und eingeht und in die Hände klatscht.

Rather not as though one should not gladly do but
Let the water have its fall
The nuts neither ripen nor do the cats take their
Tails to the grave oh no oh no don't believe so
But rather condemn without judgement
Near are the mountains they stare with their rocky
Tips delicate fingers skim them and each
Sign of love is carried away by the birds
Where to whereas the stones are stacked upon each other
Much like the rail cars in their caves
Much isn't heard but it's enough
At regular intervals the trains are drawn from
Their barrels emitting torrents of water that
Flood the fields
And the cuckoo clock strikes three but nothing
Happens just a few pellets pop out of
The fire god bless there's still deadly nightshade
Goodcherries where forgiveness and vilification
Come and go and clap their hands.

———

Toujours gai, toujours flairant le quart de vinaigre
sur la table de l'espoir.
Il est défendu aux papillons de siffler l'alarme
et aux nuages d'ouvrir les portes qui donnent
sur leurs salles noires.
L'air est pesant. Si la terre s'ouvrait maintenant,
on en verrait sortir les anges-esclaves couverts de salpêtre,
fouettés par la harpie à barbe.
Jeune homme, ne pleurez pas! Le sang ne connaît pas
de maître, le sel attire la pluie et le jour
n'est pas loin où le crime chantera dans les arbres,
où la peste en robe de chambre nous aidera
à défendre nos droits.

———

Immer munter, immer das Viertel Weinessig auf dem
Tisch der Hoffnung witternd.
Es ist den Schmetterlingen verboten, Alarm zu pfeifen,
und den Wolken, die Türen zu öffnen, die zu ihren
schwarzen Sälen führen.
Die Luft ist schwer. Wenn die Erde sich jetzt öffnete,
entstiegen ihr die salpeterbedeckten Sklavenengel,
gepeitscht von der bärtigen Harpyie.
Weinen Sie nicht, junger Mann! Das Blut kennt keinen
Meister, das Salz zieht den Regen an, und der Tag ist
nicht fern, wo das Verbrechen in den Bäumen singen
wird, wo die Pest im Morgenmantel uns helfen wird,
unsere Rechte zu verteidigen.

Ever cheerful, ever sniffing out the flask of vinegar
on the table of hope.
It's forbidden for the butterflies to sound the alarm,
for the clouds to open the doors
to their dark rooms.
The air is heavy. If the earth were to open,
enslaved angels caked in saltpeter would emerge,
beaten by the bearded harpy.
Do not weep, young man! Blood knows no
master, salt bedecks itself with rain and the day
is not distant where crime will sing amid the trees,
where the plague in its dressing gown will help us
defend our rights.

———

Je sens mon œil se tourner vers les forêts
et la lune.
Je sens ma boussole se diriger vers ces
proverbes nourrissants.
Mais mon beau crocodile
mon crocodile en cœur –
Où va ta fierté?

———

Ich spüre, wie sich mein Auge den Wäldern
und dem Mond zuwendet.
Ich fühle meinen Kompaß sich gegen diese
nahrhaften Sprichwörter richten.
Aber mein schönes Krokodil
Mein Krokodil aus Herz –
Wohin geht dein Stolz?

I feel my gaze make its way to the forest
and the moon.
I feel my compass bearing towards these
nourishing proverbs.
And yet—my beautiful crocodile,
crocodile of my heart,
where is your pride headed to?

———

Les prés et la forêt ne sont presque plus visibles,
la brume cache les champs où des moissons oubliées
laissent tomber leurs graines. Le soleil de la nuit s'allonge
sur un nuage couleur de miel.
Sa main de squelette pend et les ondes
de l'ombre passent par ses doigts. A la lisière du bois
un chasseur égaré demande aux cerfs un verre d'eau.
Tout est si calme.

———

Die Wiesen und der Wald sind fast nicht mehr sichtbar,
der Nebel verbirgt die Felder, wo vergessene Ernten
ihre Körner fallen lassen. Die Nachtsonne legt sich auf
eine honigfarbene Wolke.
Ihre Skeletthand hängt herab, und durch ihre Finger
fließen die Wellen des Schattens. Am Waldrand bittet
ein verirrter Jäger die Hirsche um ein Glas Wasser.
Alles ist so still.

———

The forest and fields are no longer visible, nearly,
the mist hides the meadows where forgotten crops
drop their seeds. The evening sun reposes
on a honey-colored cloud,
dangling its skeletal hand as shadowy
waves pass through its fingers. At the edge of the woods
a lost hunter asks the deer for a glass of water.
Stillness abounds.

Sommer

Der Löwe stützt seine Nase auf den Tischrand
Zu seiner Rechten und zu seiner Linken
Schweben zwei Nymphen
Die ihm mit weißen Federn die Wangen kitzeln
In seine Augen sind Käfige eingebaut
In den Käfigen lachen die Hexen
Mit ihren Fasanenaugen
Mit ihren Pfauenwimpern
Mit ihren weißen Haaren
Mit ihren steinernen Brüsten
Der Löwe lacht
Und sein goldenes Gebiß leuchtet
Von Sonnenaufgang bis Sonnenuntergang.

Summer

The lion rests his nose on the table's edge
Two nymphs float
To his right and left
Tickling his cheeks with white feathers
His eyes are fitted with cages
In these cages the witches are laughing
With their pheasant eyes
Their peacock lashes
Their white hair
And stony chests
The lion laughs
And his golden teeth gleam
From sunrise to sunset.

Herbst

Der Vogel platzt geräuschlos und aus seinem Bauch steigt
Ein Springbrunnen braungoldener Federn
Die Pilze lösen sich vom Boden und schweben
Von der warmen Luft getragen
Bis an die Wolken
In den Wolken lachen die Hexen
Mit ihren Fasanenaugen
Mit ihren Pfauenwimpern
Mit ihren weißen Haaren
Mit ihren steinernen Brüsten.

Fall

Without a peep the bird bursts and from its belly emerges
A fountain of golden-brown feathers
The mushrooms break away from the ground and float
Carried away by the warm air
Till they reach the clouds
In the clouds the witches are laughing
With their pheasant eyes
Their peacock lashes
Their white hair
And stony chests.

——

Oh große Ränder an meiner Zukunft Hut!

Wie sprießen die Blumen, der Himmel wälzt sich im Meer.
Die Fische tragen seinen Schleier, und ohne die Korallen zu
verletzen, eilen sie hurtig von Stein zu Stein und saugen den
Quallen ihren Honig aus, um ihn auf ungehobelten Brettern
ihrem König darzubringen. Seine goldnen Tressen klettern
an ihm auf und ab, die Ringe rollen um sein breites Haupt,
seine Füße werden von seinen Händen liebkost, und die
Sonne selbst erwärmt sein Herz.

———

Oh, magnificent brims on my future hat!

How the flowers spring up, the sky waltzes into the sea. The fish wear their veils, and, without harming the coral, nimbly rush from stone to stone, sucking the jellyfish of their honey in order to present it on raw boards to their king. His golden plaits climb up and down around him, the ringlets encircling his broad head, feet caressed by his hands, the sun itself bringing warmth to his heart.

Mit dem Radau-Gott um die Welt
Fische an den Sohlen
Flossen am Absatz
Die goldne Sonne in der Mitte.

Sein Herz bekränzt mit Efeu
Sein Gesicht gefüllt mit roten Beeren
Seine nächsten Hände liegen auf den Felsen.

Wenn er die Spur verliert
Flüchtet er zum Abgrund
Und läßt alle Löffel fallen.

———

Around the world with the hooligod
Fish on his soles
Fins on his heels
In the center, the golden sun.

His heart is covered in ivy
His face stuffed with red berries
His closest hands rest on the cliffs.

When he loses track of things
He rushes into the abyss,
Letting go of every last spoon.

Ob er steigt
Ob er sinkt
Er begegnet ihnen
Er ist unter ihnen
Ganz glänzend sind sie
Leuchtend, phosphoreszierend.

———

Whether he swims
Or sinks
He will encounter them
He is among them
Radiant as they are
Shining, phosphorescent.

—

La rosée sur la rose
Qui l'a touché avant
Avant la nuit?
Elle a gardé sa chair
Sa cire
Blanche et noire
Elle reparaît dans les nuages
Mangeant du massepain.

—

Der Tau auf der Rose
Wer berührte sie vorher
Vor der Nacht?
Sie behielt ihr bleiches Fleisch
Ihr Wachs
Weiß und schwarz
Sieht man sie wieder in den Wolken
Marzipan essend.

The dew on the rose
Who touched her before
Before night fell?
She kept her flesh
Her wax
White and black
She reappears in the clouds
Munching on marzipan.

Quelle belle femme
Somnambule
Avec son éventail
Qui sert d'éventail
Appuyée au tronc d'Hercule.

———

Welch schöne Frau
Nachtwandlerin
Mit ihrem Fächer
Der als Fächer dient
Angelehnt an den Stamm des Herkules.

Dieses Gedicht wurde provoziert
durch einen kleinen Wattebausch,
den ich in den Fingern drehte.

—

What a beautiful woman
Somnambulant
With her fan
Made to fan
Leaning against the trunk of Hercules.

This poem was provoked
by twiddling a little wad of cotton
around my fingers.

Alles verkehrt
Kreuz und quer
Auf bleichen Wegen
In trüben Nächten
Das letzte Gestirn
Sein Fuß stößt an die Honigquelle
Kreuz und quer
Alles verkehrt
Das letzte Wort hat goldene Strahlen.

Das letzte Wort
Das letzte Wort
Es reicht sich die Hände
Es setzt sich auf drei Stühle
Aus gefallenen Worten macht es ein dichtes Netz
Ein doppeltes Netz
Ein vielfaches Netz
Und stülpt es dem –
Wem?
Wer ist das?
Ich kenne ihn nicht.

Sie haben ihn gefangen
Sie tragen ihn auf eine bessere Weide
Er wartet auf den Abend und den Morgen
Er zieht die roten Vorhänge von den Wäldern
Er wandelt durch das Labyrinth der Blätterwirbel.

Er geht durch den Hohlweg
Rechts fallen die Steine
Und links fallen die Steine

Everything bungled
Mangled and jumbled
Down faded paths
On murky nights
The last celestial body
Stubs its toe against the honey well
Mangled and jumbled
Everything bungled
The final word emits golden rays.

The final word
The final word
Clasps its hands
It sits on three chairs
It makes a dense web of fallen words
A two-layer web
A multilayer web
And wraps it around—
Who?
Who's there?
I know him not.

He's been caught
Put out to greener pastures
Waiting for evening and morning
He draws the red curtains from the woods
Wandering through the maze of swirling leaves.

He moves through the gorge
Rocks falling to his right
And rocks falling to his left

Vielleicht weht der Ostwind
Vielleicht weht der Südwind
Er sieht sich um –
Graue Wüste ringsherum
Das Meer liegt erfroren am Strand
Die Statuen fallen ohnmächtig zur Erde
Tausend Blitze suchen verzweifelt den Ausgang
Die Wolken – schwarz gebläht am Horizont
Messer fliegen wie Vögel durch die Luft.

Nichts mehr zu hören
Nichts zu sehen
Nichts zu fühlen.

Er hat sich selbst vergessen
Er lebt in einem Schneeflockenmeer
In der Schneeglockenkammer
Unsichtbar.

Auf grünen Fahnen fährt er davon
Er stößt die Tore ein
Die Diener stehn in Flammen
Bekränzte Wände und gewürzte Speisen
In Ritterrüstung tafeln die erschlagnen Bräute
Die zarten Finger schmelzen auf den Tellern
Und ihre Lippen saugen gierig
Die wohlgenährten Putten aus
Die sie umarmen und wie Katzen schnurren
Bis ihre Larvenhaut zu Boden fällt.

Wenn der gefleckte Mond verschwunden ist
Und die Flötentöne schwächer werden
Und Morgennebel durch die Fenster dringt

Maybe it's the east wind blowing
Maybe it's the south wind blowing
He is looking around—
The gray wasteland about
The sea lies frozen on the beach
The statues fall fainting to the earth
A thousand lightning bolts search for the exit in despair
The clouds, black and bloated on the horizon
Knives fly like birds through the air.

Nothing more to hear
Nothing to see
Nothing to feel.

He's lost track of himself
He lives in a snowflakesea
Invisible
In the snowquakechamber.

He sails away on green flags
smashing through the gates
The servants are in flames
Garlanded walls and spiced dishes
Slain brides feast in suits of armor
Their delicate fingers melting on the plates
And their greedy lips suck dry
The well-fed cherubs
Who clutch and purr at them like cats
Till their larval skin falls to the ground.

When the pocked moon has vanished
And the music of the flute subsides
And the morning fog is pressing through the windows

Dann zerspringen die Gläser und die perlmuttrigen Blasen
Die Tränen fließen in die Bäche zurück
Und das Moos trocknet auf den Steinen
Wenn die Sonne ihren Fächer öffnet.

The glassware and pearly globules will shatter
The tears flowing back into the streams
The moss drying out on the stones
As the sun fans open.

Edelfuchs im Morgenrot
Spinnt sein Netz im Abendrot
Schädlich ist der Widerschein
Schädlich sind die Nebenmotten
Ohne sie kann nichts gedeihn.

The fine fox in the glow of dawn
Spins his web in the glow of dusk
Baneful is the reflection
Baneful are the additional suns
Without which nothing thrives.

———

Ohne mich ohnehin ohne Weg kam ich dahin ohne Brot
ohne Atem aber mitnichten mitneffen mit Kaspar
mit Kuchen so rund war er etwas eckig zwar
aber ohne Grasbewuchs mit Narben mit Warzen mit Fingern
mit Stäben mit vielen O's und wenig W's
dafür mit ganz enorm wenig viel.
Oh falle du doch in dein Loch oh begrabe du dich doch selbst
und deine langatmige Hoffnung
gib deinem Ich einen Tritt deinem Es seinen Lohn
und was von dir übrig bleibt brate wie Fischlein im Öl
du kannst deine Schuhe abstreifen.

———

Without me anyway without a way I came up without bread
without breath but by no means with kin with Kaspar
with cake he was so round a bit angular even
but without swaths of grass with scars with warts with fingers
with rods with lots of O's and not much by way of W's
and so with a massive amount of not much.
Oh now go fall down in your hole oh go bury yourself
and your longwinded hope
give your ego a kick your id its due
and what remains of you fry like the fishies in oil
you can wipe your shoes.

Sansibar

Weil er sich den Rücken kehrt
Verliert er
Über den Kaminen
Die roten Ecklein
Die roten Füchslein
Alle leben einsam
Sie zehren am längsten
Sie essen ihren Pelz.

Zanzibar

As he's turned his back
He's lost
Above the chimneys
The little red corners
The little red foxes
All live forlorn
They ever endure
They eat their fur.

Hörst du die Löwen brüllen
Vereint verbannt verzehrt
Der Tag hat sie geschlagen
Ohne Wiederkehr.

Do you hear the lions roaring
United exiled exhausted
The day has struck them
Without turning back.

Dein Rhombengesicht. Viereck, Dreieck. Grünrotes,
im Wasser versunkenes. Die Gräser drumherum, es sinkt,
sinkt bis zum Licht auf dem Grund, Flieder blüht, Flieder
    flieht.
Durch die Brille sieht man die Löwen fliehn.
Eintracht, schwarze Nacht. Rotes Licht, roter Kreis,
rotes Viereck.
Quer drüber zieht hellblauer Frühlingshimmel.
Darin Züge von schwarzen Vögeln, die mit den weißen
    Wolken
fliegen. Insektenschwärme.

———

Your rhomboid face: rectangular, triangular, red-green
submerged in water. Amid the grass and all the rest, it's
    sinking,
sinking to the light at the bottom. Lilacs blossom, lilacs flee.
Through one's spectacles one sees the lions flee.
Oneness, black night. Red light, red circle,
red square.
The pale blue spring sky stretches overhead.
Flocks of black birds inside, together with the white clouds
they fly. Swarms of insects.

Oh Traurigkeit. Versunken in den blauschwarzen
Gruben dunkel glänzender Blätter. Umstellt mich,
Finstere Gestalten. Rote Glut glimmt. Glücklicher
Vollmond streckt die Arme aus. Gefährlich weiße
Wolke zieht. Schwarze Wolke streckt ihr die
Zunge heraus. In den Schluchten Qualm und
Riesige Tierleiber rollen. Wenigstens Wasser,
Flechten, Moos, alles tropft Silbertau.
Es sind nicht Engel, es sind Feen,
Die vorbeifliegen mit hellen Schenkeln.
Sie streifen die Gebüsche.
Ich fröstle in der Morgenkälte.

Oh, sadness. Sunk in the blue-black grooves
Of the dark gleaming leaves. Dark figures,
Surround me. Red embers glow. Merry
Full moon extends its arms, dangerous white cloud
Departs, black cloud sticks its tongue
Out. Smoke and immense animal bodies
Roil in the ravines. Water, lichen, moss, at least
Everything drips with silver dew.
They are not angels—they are fairies,
Flying by with bright thighs,
Grazing the bushes.
I shiver in the morning cold.

Ich muß die schwarzen Worte der Schwäne
aufschreiben. Die goldene Karosse am Ende der Allee
teilt sich, fällt um und schmilzt auf der
regenfeuchten Straße.
Eine Wolke bunter Schmetterlinge fliegt auf und
erfüllt den Himmel mit ihrem Getön.
Ach, das rote Fleisch und die blauen Kleeblätter,
sie gehen Hand in Hand.

I must take note of the swans'
black words. At the avenue's end, the golden coach
splits in half, collapsing and melting onto
the road wet from rain.
A cloud of colorful butterflies flits away,
filling the skies with their clangor.
Oh, the red meat and blue clovers
go hand in hand with one another.

——

Ein merkwürdiger Erdteil in
Weiße Tücher gewickelt
Rollt die gewundene Treppe
Eines Hauses hinunter
Man rollt ihn (Zeremonie)
Die gewundene
Treppe eines Hauses hinunter
Pulvrig ungesehen bleibt er auf der Straße liegen
    Nachts ein helles Relief
    Mühsam
Wie eine bergige Landschaft.

A peculiar continent
Swaddled in white cloth
Rolls down the building's
Winding stairs
You roll it (ceremony)
Down the winding
Stairs of the building
Powdery unseen it remains there on the street
    At night in bright relief
    Painstaking
Like a mountainous landscape.

In der Juninacht
zirpen die Grillen
und der Liguster blüht.
Weiß-und-grün heißt der Liguster
und duftet süß
an der staubigen Straße
im trockenen Flußbett.

In der Juninacht
Wetterleuchten wie Wellen
am Ufer des Himmels.
Jammer und Drohung –
Wer ruft um Hilfe?
Ein Tal voller Blitze
jenseits der Berge.

In the twilit June
the crickets chirp
and the privet blooms:
a white and green privet
with sweet perfume
on a dusty road
in a dry riverbed.

In the twilit June
along the sky's edge
wavelike lightning looms:
anguish and menace—
is anyone calling for help?
A valley rife with flashes
beyond the mountains.

Schwach, schwächer, links.
Die Lebenden links.
Die Toten voran.
Der Störrische wird bald sich nahn.

Wer einmal pfeift, gehört nicht her.
Er wird gesiebt, geachtet
Und neun und gut geschlachtet
Und endlich sind die Haare leer.

Weak and weaker to the left.
Same for the living.
The dead, straight ahead.
The restive will soon draw near.

Whoever whistles doesn't belong here.
They'll be severed, attended,
Nine and well butchered
And in the end, bare of hair.

Endlich

Der Metzgerhund schnappt nach dem goldenen Ring.
Die Fee ist gut, aber der Kaffee hart und der
Granit weichgekocht wie eine Haube aus Katzenfell.
Die Knaben, die Männer, die Greise.
Sie sitzen auf der Mauer und beraten. Sie deuten in der
Runde. Die Pflastersteine springen aus dem Boden
wie Springbrunnen und machen sich in alle
Richtungen davon. Man könnte sagen, etwas stimme
nicht. Aber es sind nur die geheimen Kräfte,
die man schon seit heute früh erwartet. Die Steine
fliegen bis zur Küste des Nordmeeres, wo sie an
den silberglänzenden Fäden hängen bleiben.
Sie schaukeln in der Morgensonne.

Finally

The Rottweiler snaps at the golden ring.
The fairy is good but the coffee hard, the
granite soft-boiled as a cover of cat fur.
Boys, men, old men.
They sit on the wall, deliberating. Taking turns
offering their explanations. The cobblestones spring up
from the ground like fresh springs and make off in all
directions. You could say that something is
wrong. But it's just the secret forces
you've been waiting for since dawn. The stones
fly all the way to the north seacoast where they
get caught in silvery threads,
swaying in the morning sun.

Zartäugige Wandelgänge essen Butter am
laufenden Band. Wieviel verspricht er dir.
Solothurn. Solothurn. Die Braut von Solothurn
verteilt Fledermäuse unter das hungrige Volk.

Bleary-eyed boardwalks eat butter
round the clock. He promises you how much.
Solothurn. Solothurn. The Bride of Solothurn
dispenses bats to the hungry folk.

Ebenso wertvoll aber sind die vergessenen Nachtigallen die
die granitenen Suppen essen und auf ihre Zeit warten.
»Das rote Licht leuchtet auf und alles.«

———

Nevertheless they matter, too, the forgotten nightingales
eating granitic soup and biding their time.
The red light turns on, everything.

———

Wohin führt der Wagen?
Der Wagen führt in den Wald. Der Wald
gehört dem Winterkoller.
Wie erfährt man seine Adresse?
Man dreht die Türe um.
Man liest die Lobhymnen der Zugvögel, der
Wasserfische, der verdammten und verfluchten
Pustakäfer.

Hier herrscht kein Kastengeist.
Hier darf sich jeder ungehindert äußern.
Wer Heu im Arm hat, darf es verspeisen.
Lebend oder tot macht man seine Reverenz.
Langsam naht das Alter. Aber es kann dich
nicht unterscheiden.
Du verbirgst dich hinter einem Nachtschmetterling,
der sein schönstes Mimikri macht
und dir seinen Schlaf opfert.

Where is the carriage heading?
The carriage is heading to the woods. The woods
belong to the ravages of winter.
How to come upon its address?
You turn round the door; you
read the hymns of the migrating birds, the
water fish, the condemned and cursed
Puszta beetles.

Here, no spirit of fellow feeling rules.
Here, all may express themselves freely.
Whoever is armed with hay may eat it.
Living or dead you pay your respects.
Age creeps up. But it cannot
tell you apart.
You hide behind a moth
making its finest mimicry,
sacrificing sleep for you.

———

Kacherache, panache,
Lob dem schüchternen Wallachen.
Langsam naht er – kommt oder kommt nicht.
Aber sicher ist, daß man ihn übersieht.
So verlangts der gute Ton.

Ich kenne ihn.
Er reicht dir die Hand zum Gruß und zieht sie
nicht zurück, obwohl sie stinkt. Auf der Straße
beißt er dich in die Wade.
Der Königin von England hat er ein Taschentuch geschenkt.

Wir wollen lebenslänglich Stühle flechten.

Kacherache, panache,
Praise the shy gelding.
He's approaching slowly, he's coming or not.
But without a doubt is overlooked.
As good form requires.

I recognize him.
He greets you with his outstretched hand and
despite its stench does not withdraw it,
nipping at your calves on the street.
To the queen of England he gave a kerchief.

Our lifelong wish is to take to twining chairs.

Der Hund meiner Freundin

Ich liebe den Hund meiner
Freundin. Er kann so schön
»ja« sagen. Er sagt »ja«, wenn
man ihn vergißt. Er verdammt
keinen, der sich mit ihm vergleicht.
Wo er hinkommt, da kehrt der
Frühling ein. Weint er, verliert
die Natur ihre Federn. Ist er
hingegen wohlgelaunt, schiebt
er mit viel Geschick die Hand zum
Mund, um ihm seine tiefsten
Geheimnisse abzulauschen.
Wie jeder brave Mann hat er
zwei Seelen in jeder Brust,
fünfundzwanzig an Händen und Füßen.

My Girlfriend's Dog

I adore my girlfriend's dog.
He has such a lovely way of
saying "yes." He says "yes"
when he's forgotten. And
has no harsh words for those
who compare themselves to him.
Spring sets up shop wherever
he goes. If he cries, nature
loses its plumes. If he happens to be
in a good mood, he tactfully
brings a hand to his mouth
to eavesdrop on its deepest secrets.
Like every good being he has
two souls in each chest and
twenty-five in hand and foot.

Dort oben in jenem Garten
Dort stehen meine Schatten
Die mir den Rücken kühlen.

Sie stehen in dem Garten
Sie streiten um ein altes Brot
Und krähen wie die Hähne.

Heut will ich sie besuchen
Heut will ich sie begrüßen
Und ihre Nasen zählen.

Over there in that garden
There lie my shadows
That cool my back.

They're up in the garden
Squabbling over old bread
And clucking like chickens.

Today I want to visit them
Today I want to greet them
And number their noses.

Verlassen, vergessen –
So schwarz am Haferstrand.
Ich will die Zeit nicht messen,
Die diesen Schmerz erfand.

Die gelben Wellen schlagen
Das neue Netz entzwei.
Sie kommen, gehn und sagen:
Das arme Allerlei!

Forgotten, abandoned,
So black amid the beachgrass.
I don't want to measure how
Time brought this pain to pass.

The mauve waves rip
The new net asunder.
They come, go, and quip,
"What a sorry jumble!"

Die Arche Noah

Immer mehr und weniger
Salz am Knie und Wachs am Kopf –
Warum trinkst du nicht, mein Lieber?
Sieh, schon wächst der Baum im Kropf.

Nimm die Schöne aus dem Wasser,
Trockne ihre nasse Hand
Und vergieß die schwarzen Algen
In den eisernen Bestand.

Noah's Ark

Always more and always less
Salt on the knee and wax up top—
My love, why aren't you drinking?
Look, a tree is growing in the gullet.

Fetch the beauty from the water,
Dry her wet hand and
Cast the black algæ
Into an iron existence.

Wer ihre weißen Finger sieht, ist bereit, sich zu
verwandeln. Alle entsteigen ihrer Haut, um sich der
neuen Welt hinzugeben. Alle wissen, daß kein Schiff
sie zurückbringt, aber das Füllhorn winkt. Es öffnet
seine Fächer und läßt seinen Duft ausströmen. Die
grünen Vögel zerreißen die Segel, und die große
Sonne fällt ins Wasser. Aber solange einer die
Trommel rührt, kann die Nacht nicht sinken.
Der Himmel ist gelb, das Meer ist grau.

Die Fahrt dauert schon über hundert Jahre. Die
Menschen schwimmen wie Haifische um ihr Schiff,
und das Meer ist rot von Blut. Nur die braunen Hunde
strecken die Köpfe über den Schiffsrand. Sie halten
kleine Messer im Maul und lassen sie von Zeit zu Zeit
auf die Menschen unter ihnen fallen. Die Messer
bleiben in der Sonne stecken, die tief unten auf dem
Meeresgrund liegt. Die Sonne bekommt
kleine Flossen.

Whoever regards their white fingers is ready to be
transformed. Everyone steps out of their skin
to surrender themselves to the new world. They all know
no ship will bring them back though the horn of plenty beckons.
It unfurls its array, letting the aromas emanate. The
green birds shred the sails, the massive
sun drops into the water. But so long as the
drum beats on, night cannot fall.
The sky is yellow; the ocean, gray.

The journey has taken more than a hundred years.
People swim around their ship like sharks
and the sea is red with blood. Only the brown dogs
stick their necks out beyond the railing, clutching
small knives in their mouths, which they let drop
from time to time on the people down below. The knives
transfix the sun stranded on the
ocean floor. The sun is growing
little fins.

Kein Keim. Schlacken knistern unter dem Fuß.
Am Horizont rote Sonne oder ist es Feuerschein.
Alle Augen sind geschlossen. Die Helme liegen am
Boden. Wo sind die Träume hin? Hin und her treibt
der Wind schwarze Ufer um ein Wasser, in dem sich heller
Himmel spiegelt, Fragen steigen auf.
Das Gelächter der Fledermäuse.

No new life. Cinders crackle underfoot.
A red sun on the horizon or is it the glow of fire.
Everyone's eyes are closed. The helmets lie
on the floor. Where have dreams gone to? The wind
drives black banks back and forth across the water,
in its sheen a bright sky, questions arise.
The laughter of bats.

Getreuer Kapitän
Sage es mir
Zeige mir die Stelle in den Wolken
Die der Flügel der Schwalbe öffnete
Das Wellental in den Haaren der Göttin
Die grünen Lichter im Wald.

Hier ist Nacht –
Böse Besen erschlagen die Kobolde
Kein Rad dreht sich mehr.

Das Dunkel kennt sich nicht
Es fragt auch nicht
Es ist eine Faust in einer Faust
Die niemand sieht.

Faithful captain
Tell me
Show me the place in the clouds
Where the swallow's wing opened
The wavelike trough in the goddess's hair
The green lights in the forest.

Now it is night.
Wicked shrews whack the goblins
The wheels have stopped turning

The darkness knows itself not—
It doesn't even bother to ask.
It is a fist within a fist
Seen by no one.

—

Heiße Hand auf kühlem Eisengitter
Perlmutterne Statue
Wie zieht es mich zu dir
Perlmutterne Statue
Deine Locken sind starr
Und dein Gewand
Ist vom Nachtwind unbewegt.

———

Hot hand on the cool iron fence
Mother-of-pearl statue
What draws me to you
Mother-of-pearl statue
Your curls are fixed
And your robe unmoved
By the evening wind.

Am Anfang ist das Ende
der Vulkan überhäuft uns mit Geschenken
wie traurig waren wir
der Himmel tropft auf die Teller
das Gras sinkt herab mit Tau bedeckt
Halleluja Schabernack und kein Ende
die Schelmen blasen die Schelmei
zaghaft liegen die Wasserrosen und schlagen
die Augen auf und zu
die Reusen sind leer
der schwarze Sack ist voll
was dem Apfel die Kerne sind der Erde die Ameisen
kein Geräusch ist hörbar nur die Mondsichel steht am Himmel
das Feuerwerk knallt und die Nacht ist paillettenübersät.

In the beginning is the end
the volcano showered us with gifts
how sad we were
the sky drips on the plates
the grass sinks down covered in dew
hallelujah antics without end
fools blowing flutes
the waterlilies lie tentatively beating
their eyes open and closed
the traps are empty
the black sack is full
as seeds to the apple are ants to the earth
no sound is heard only the crescent moon hangs in the sky
fireworks pop and the night is sequinstrewn.

———

Ich bin ein Wickelkind
Gewickelt mit eisernem Griff.

———

I am a swaddling child
Swaddled in an iron grip.

Selbstportrait seit 50 000 v.Chr. bis X

Meine Füße stehen auf von vielen Schritten
abgerundeten Steinen in einer Tropfsteinhöhle. Ich lasse
mir das Bärenfleisch schmecken. Mein Bauch ist von
einer warmen Meeresströmung umflossen, ich stehe in
den Lagunen, mein Blick fällt auf die rötlichen Mauern
einer Stadt. Brustkorb und Arme stecken in einem
Panzer aus dicht übereinandergenähten Lederschuppen.
In den Händen halte ich eine Schildkröte aus weißem
Marmor. In meinem Kopf sind die Gedanken
eingeschlossen wie in einem Bienenkorb.
Später schreibe ich sie nieder. Die Schrift ist verbrannt,
als die Bibliothek von Alexandrien brannte. Die
schwarze Schlange mit dem weißen Kopf steht im
Museum in Paris. Dann verbrennt auch sie. Alle
Gedanken, die je gedacht wurden, rollen um die Erde in
der großen Geistkugel. Die Erde zerspringt, die
Geistkugel platzt, die Gedanken zerstreuen sich im
Universum, wo sie auf andern Sternen
weiterleben.

Self-Portrait from 50,000 B.C. to X

My feet stand up on stones rounded
by many steps in a craggy cave. I let
myself enjoy the bear meat. My belly
is bathed by a warm ocean current, I
stand in the lagoons, my gaze lands on a city's
reddened walls. Arms and ribcage are stuck
in armor made of tightly sewn leather scales.
In my hands I hold a turtle made of white
marble. My thoughts are shut away
inside my head as in a beehive.
I'll write them down later. The script was burned
when the library at Alexandria burned. The
black snake with the white head is located in
the museum in Paris. It too will burn. Each and every
thought that has ever been thunk rolls round the earth
in the great spiritsphere. The earth cracks, the
spiritsphere bursts, thoughts disperse in the
universe, where they on other stars
live on.

Acknowledgments

The translator wishes to thank Vickie Kennedy, Steve Thompson, Margaret Pearce, Nora Mercurio and Elena Cascio at Suhrkamp, Lisa Wenger of the Estate of Meret Oppenheim, Nadja Prenzel and the Deutscher Übersetzerfonds for their support, Elisa Heine for her thoughts on an early draft of the translations, Matvei Yankelevich and the editorial team at World Poetry, and the editors and staff of the following publications where several of these translations first appeared, sometimes in earlier forms: *Arkansas International*, *Circumference*, *New England Review*, *The New Yorker*, *The Paris Review*, and *World Poetry Review*.

Meret Oppenheim was born in Berlin in 1913 and died in Basel in 1985. Best known for *Object*, her fur-lined teacup from 1936, her expansive body of work included painting, works on paper, sculpture, object constructions, jewelry designs, and poetry.

Kathleen Heil is a writer/translator and choreographer/performer whose poetry, prose, and translations appear in *The New Yorker*, *Fence*, *Two Lines*, *The Threepenny Review*, and other journals.

This book is typeset in Sabon with Söhne titling.

German typographer Jan Tschichold designed Sabon in 1964, combining types by the great French punch-cutters of the sixteenth century: Claude Garamond and Robert Granjon. Sabon is named for Jakob Sabon, a student who carried on Garamond's work after his death in 1561.

Released in 2019, Kris Sowersby's Söhne—German for "sons"—is in the lineage of Akzidenz-Grotesk, the first sans-serif typeface to gain broad usage, which dates to 1896 and is the basis for Helvetica. Söhne attempts to retain its forebear's analogue materiality and avoid strict rationalization.

The artwork on the cover is a self-portrait by Meret Oppenheim from 1964, titled "X-Ray of M.O.'s Skull." Cover design by Andrew Bourne; typesetting by Don't Look Now. Printed and bound by KOPA in Lithuania.

⊕⊕⊕ WORLD POETRY

Jean-Paul Auxeméry
Selected Poems
tr. Nathaniel Tarn

Maria Borio
Transparencies
tr. Danielle Pieratti

Jeannette L. Clariond
Goddesses of Water
tr. Samantha Schnee

Jacques Darras
John Scotus Eriugena at Laon
tr. Richard Sieburth

Olivia Elias
Chaos, Crossing
tr. Kareem James Abu-Zeid

Phoebe Giannisi
Homerica
tr. Brian Sneeden

Zuzanna Ginczanka
On Centaurs and Other Poems
tr. Alex Braslavsky

Nakedness Is My End:
Poems from the Greek Anthology
tr. Edmund Keeley

Jazra Khaleed
The Light That Burns Us
ed. Karen Van Dyck

Jerzy Ficowski
Everything I Don't Know
tr. Jennifer Grotz & Piotr Sommer
PEN AWARD FOR POETRY IN TRANSLATION

Antonio Gamoneda
Book of the Cold
tr. Katherine M. Hedeen &
Víctor Rodríguez Núñez

Maria Laina
Hers
tr. Karen Van Dyck

Maria Laina
Rose Fear
tr. Sarah McCann

Perrin Langda
A Few Microseconds on Earth
tr. Pauline Levy Valensi

Manuel Maples Arce
Stridentist Poems
tr. KM Cascia

Enio Moltedo
Night
tr. Marguerite Feitlowitz

Meret Oppenheim
The Loveliest Vowel Empties:
Collected Poems
tr. Kathleen Heil

Elisabeth Rynell
Night Talks
tr. Rika Lesser

Giovanni Pascoli
Last Dream
tr. Geoffrey Brock
RAIZISS/DE PALCHI TRANSLATION AWARD

Rainer Maria Rilke
Where the Paths Do Not Go
tr. Burton Pike

Ardengo Soffici
Simultaneities & Lyric Chemisms
tr. Olivia E. Sears

Ye Lijun
My Mountain Country
tr. Fiona Sze-Lorrain

Verónica Zondek
Cold Fire
tr. Katherine Silver